THE AFTER PARTY

DEVOTIONAL COMPANION

THE AFTER PARTY
DEVOTIONAL COMPANION

KATE BATTISTELLI

The After Party Devotional Companion

Welcome, Mama!

I'm thrilled you're joining me as we jump in and take a deeper, more intimate look at your empty nest journey. Whether or not you're a brand-new empty nester, a soon-to-be empty nester, or you've been in your empty nest for a while now, I understand how challenging and bittersweet the struggle can be, but I am confident you can get through it. The empty nest doesn't have to overwhelm you or cause you to plunge into a pit of despair. Through this *The After Party of the Empty Nest* companion journal and devotional, we'll walk together for thirty-one days as we lean into God's promises, listen for His voice, and find purpose in His plan. There is a future with your name on it! *Your empty nest doesn't have to be an empty mess.*

"Kintsugi (joining with gold) is the Japanese art of repairing broken pottery with lacquer dusted or mixed with powdered gold, silver, or platinum. The vicissitudes of existence over time, to which all humans are susceptible, could not be clearer than in the breaks, the knocks, and the shattering to which ceramic ware is subject. As a philosophy, it treats breakage and repair as part of the history of an object, rather than something to disguise." Christy Bartlett[1]

---

1   "Kintsugi – Art of Repair" by Christy Bartlett. Source: TraditionalKyoto. com. https://traditionalkyoto.com/culture/kintsugi/

"The breaks, the knocks, and the shattering." Describes the empty nest quite accurately! How many of us feel broken, knocked, and even shattered when our children leave the nest? We don't believe we will ever be put back together the way we were, but we know one thing for sure: we will never be the same. And, in fact, we won't. That's the philosophy behind Kintsugi. Think of it as God repairing the breaks with golden lines that embrace our frailty, highlighting our imperfections and turning them into art rather than hiding them.

Kintsugi reminds me to keep my eyes on what's possible and chase after peace when life falls apart. It teaches me to accept my scars and flaws, my mistakes and shortcomings, cracked and put back together. God will use those shattered pieces of our lives and reconnect them, cracks and all, with beautiful veins of silver and gold.

Some days, when your life feels like broken pottery, you try to pick up the pieces and put them back together yourself, but the task seems impossible. All those feelings bubbling up inside are entirely natural and to be expected. But they don't have to hijack your peace or snatch away your purpose. Your future is at stake, the plan God has had for you since the foundation of the world. Your part? Dig deep with Jesus, spend time in His presence, and pray to understand where He is leading you in this new era of life. Jump in. Pick up those cracked parts and hand them to Jesus so He can line them with gold. He alone can craft your life into something beautiful to behold.

How does all that apply to those navigating an empty nest?

My goal with this companion devotional journal is to provide a practical tool to help you embrace your empty nest as a sacred opportunity for growth, renewal, and discovering your new purpose now that your kids have moved into adulthood. I pray it helps you define your feelings as you meditate on the daily scripture and write down your thoughts, plans, and emotions as you grapple with your specific empty nest story in the journal pages. Journaling is a fantastic way to wrestle with our questions, thoughts, frustrations, answers to prayer, resonating scriptures, and more. And those places where regret has left us scarred? That too will be artfully addressed as you lean on the One who redeems and repairs.

You aren't here by mistake. The Lord is handing you a holy invitation to a future designed *specifically* for you. As you begin to think it through, your eyes will open, giving you a different view and a fresh sense of excitement as you enter this brand-new stage of life. Even if only one or some of your children have left home, you likely feel many of the same emotions as the mom whose last child has moved out. Now is the time to begin preparing for the next stage of life, examining and planning for your future as you continue your season of active mothering.

This devotional journal isn't about checking off tasks or achieving perfection. It's about diving even deeper than we could in *The After Party of the Empty Nest,* meeting God in the middle of your questions, and finding His grace for every step of the journey. Let His hands put those broken parts back together and gently seal them with gold.

How to use *The After Party Companion*:

Every day, you'll encounter:

- **A Scripture Reflection:** Daily scripture verse to anchor your heart.
- **An Encouraging Thought:** A personal message to inspire you.
- **A Journal Prompt:** Space to pour out your thoughts and prayers.
- **Goals for Today:** What to focus on right now.
- **Common Obstacle:** The primary obstacle blocking your way.

- **Overcoming the Obstacle:** Encouragement to move forward, plus strategies to help you overcome challenges.
- **A Prayer Starter:** A guide to help you pray with confidence.

Set aside time each day to examine and work through these prompts with an open heart. You don't have to rush—let God set the pace. He longs to meet you here.

DAY 1
A NEW CHAPTER

Scripture Reflection:

"For I know the plans I have for you," declares the Lord, "plans to prosper you and not to harm you, plans to give you hope and a future." Jeremiah 29:11

An Encouraging Thought:

Most of us have read the above scripture and probably know it by heart. It may be overly familiar, but its promises are true. As you begin your empty nest, you're not only leaving your child behind but the person you knew so well–the other you. There's no muscle memory when your kids leave. You are experiencing this for the first time. But, regardless of what emotions are swirling around right now, you have *not* been put out to pasture.

You can dread the changes you're experiencing or see them as opportunities for new adventures. The positive? Significantly more free time, slower mornings, opportunities to volunteer and help others, less expensive meals out, extra time to care for yourself, and your moment to learn something new. Your future and purpose didn't leave when your kids did.

It's a brand-new chapter, and God is already writing beauty into every line. You can trust His pen and heart because He is the Author of hope. You can't see the full path ahead, but you don't have to. All you need to do is take one small step at a time, knowing He is aware of the tumult of emotions you're experiencing.

In Genesis 12, when God told Abraham to leave behind everything he knew–his country, home, and family–He told him to go to a land He would *show* him. God didn't tell Abraham where he was headed. Abraham's job was to trust God and take it one day at a time, allowing God to lead the way.

It takes a brave heart to step forward down a dimly lit path. But all any of us need is to see the step right in front of us. We may not fully understand the end from the beginning, but God does. He knows precisely where He's taking you and only asks that you trust and follow.

Goal for Today:

Take a small step to embrace this new season today. Have lunch with a friend, explore a new hobby, enjoy a museum or concert, read a good book, or spend time in the Word.

Common Obstacle:

Fear of the unknown.

Overcoming the Obstacle:

We all have some apprehension, and it's natural as you come to terms with your empty nest. However, none of us want fear to take the reins of our lives. We have to fight it with everything we've got. The enemy of our souls loves to use fear as his first line of attack. But fear doesn't have to own you, my friend. *Courage is a choice.*

To obey without seeing is key, trusting that God has a plan, and His plan will change the world as we obey and follow, even when we aren't quite sure where we are going. By saying yes, Abraham changed the world. Our yes changes the world, too!

It's perfectly fine to have some trepidation about this new phase, and it's to be expected. You've never been in this stage of life before! But try this: Breathe deeply and repeat Jeremiah 29:11 aloud, embracing every word and truth in that scripture. Remember, faith comes by *hearing*. The more you say the scriptures out loud, the more they will stick in your mind as they renew it. You might not know the plans He has for you (I certainly didn't), but His plans are always good. Rest in His promises. He offers you a future and a hope. Take one brave step forward today—He's walking right beside you.

Journal Prompt:

Write about what you anticipate and your biggest concerns and fears about this brand-new season.

Prayer Starter:

Lord, thank You for guiding me through my empty nest. I know You are always with me, but I need Your help to determine my next steps...

DAY 2
THE GRIEF IS REAL

Scripture Reflection:

Blessed are those who mourn, for they shall be comforted.
Matthew 5:4

Come to Me, all you who labor and are heavy laden, and I will give you rest. Take My yoke upon you and learn from Me, for I am gentle and lowly in heart, and you will find rest for your souls. For My yoke is easy, and My burden is light. Matthew 11:28-30

Encouraging Thought:

Your house is vacant, unoccupied chairs sit empty around the table, the fridge is mostly bare, and you have the sense that life as you've always known it has ended. Like a hard and heavy pile of bricks, the truth of this new season weighs down your heart, and, as many moms experience when they hit the empty nest for the first time, you're confused and don't like it one bit. (Even if you still have kids at home, that empty place at the dinner table is a stark reminder that someone is missing.) You are and always will be Mom, but what else does God have in store? What other name does He call you? What is this "new normal" going to look like?

Many of us slog through, but it's not pretty or graceful. On some days, it's hard, with lots of tears, questions, and doubts, but it's also holding on no matter what. It's giving up control and determining to trust Jesus, the only trustworthy One. On other days, you feel entirely fragile, and it's all you can do to lie in bed watching sad romances on Netflix and crying your eyes out. Then, there are days when the light shines, and the future looks bright.

Life has forever shifted as you realize the empty nest is more complicated than you thought. The harsh reality is this: You can't go back to before, and you're forced to look at what's *there*, not what you wish was there. The hard truth hits that you didn't volunteer for this, *you were drafted.*

It's okay to be sad, Mama. You don't have to pretend to be brave and get a grip on all the emotions swirling through your mind. *You don't.* God is right there with you in the ugly cry, the questions, doubts, and fears.

However, God created you with gifts, passions, and a specific calling unique to you. Maybe they've been put on pause during the busy years of raising your children. But now, as the grief begins to ebb, it's time to both rediscover and nurture those gifts. As you can, begin to make an effort to clarify your next steps. When you do, you will gain a clearer picture of your path as excitement about your future begins to build.

Goal for Today:

Allow yourself to look back and mourn the passing of one season as you transition into the next, but open your eyes to the new path God may be offering you. He goes before you to prepare the way.

Common Obstacles:

Getting stuck in the past.

Overcoming the Obstacle:

I understand how frustrating it can be. We can let our memories drag us down into the pit of despair and self-pity, or we can choose to fight and tell the enemy he doesn't get to win. We can say, "No, sir, this is *not* how my story ends."

Grief is a hard place to park our hearts, but Jesus is there, too. Scripture tells us He is well acquainted with both grief and mourning. He will let us visit but never wants us to stay there, reminding us that in Him alone is life and peace and joy. Jesus is all we will ever need. Grief and mourning may follow us, but His goodness and mercy follow us, too, every day, sticking even closer than those other somber companions.

If you're dealing with grief today, turn to the One who can give you true hope, lift your head, and give you peace. Spend time in prayer, and imagine yourself handing each burden to Jesus and see Him carrying them for you ... because He is.

Journal Prompt:

Write a list of the realities of the season you're holding onto, the ones causing you to mourn for the past. How can you release them to God? Be honest, and don't fear writing down the hard parts, this is for God's eyes only.

Prayer Starter:

Lord, You know how much I'm struggling with grief. Show me what I can do to overcome it…

Day 3
Letting Go

Scripture Reflection:

Blessed is the man who trusts in the Lord, and whose hope is the Lord. For he shall be like a tree planted by the waters, which spreads out its roots by the river, and will not fear when heat comes; But its leaf will be green, and will not be anxious in the year of drought, nor will cease from yielding fruit. Jeremiah 17:7-8

Encouraging Thought:

Letting go is hard, especially when it feels like you're leaving behind a season that defined much of who you are. The person and role you knew so well has been refashioned into something strange and difficult to define. It's as if you are suspended in midair, wondering if you'll fly into your future or collapse exhausted on solid ground.

But life doesn't let any of us stay in one place forever. You're in a sandwich season, hanging between what was and what is right ahead of you. Just as the seasons change, so do the chapters of our lives. Isaiah 43:18-19 beautifully reminds us,

Do not remember the former things, nor consider the things of old. Behold, I will do a new thing, now it shall spring forth; Shall you not know it? I will even make a road in the wilderness and rivers in the desert.

Jesus loves to make "roads and rivers." They remind us there is a way through, and letting go doesn't mean forgetting. It means releasing your tight-fisted grip on the past so you can stretch out open hands to what God has next. Start by acknowledging what was good in your mothering season and thanking God for your years as a mom. Gratitude will turn mourning into praise as you reflect on the lessons you learned and how you grew during your active child-rearing years. It can become the foundation for your next steps. The "you" that used to be is now part of your past. There's a different you to embrace in your empty nest.

Sometimes, we hold on to the past with clenched fists because it feels safe and familiar, while the future looks hazy and hesitant. You may be reluctant to let go. But remember, *God goes before you.* He's in your tomorrow, making a way in the wilderness, preparing your path, and equipping you for what's to come.

Ask the Lord for the courage to move forward, even though the path may be shadowed and dimly lit. Faith often means stepping into the dark, trusting that God will show you the way in His perfect timing. Surround yourself with people who encourage and challenge you to grow, their prayers and support can help you lay hold of what's ahead.

Finally, lean into God's promises because He's not finished with you, not by any means. What may feel like an ending can become the beginning of something beautiful, and as you allow your heart to embrace the new episode God is unfolding, you'll find His plans are always good, faithful, and always filled with hope.

Goal for Today:

Surrender your heartache to God in prayer.

Common Obstacle:

The tendency to stay stuck in the past.

Overcoming the Obstacle:

Releasing your identity as a mom might feel like losing a part of yourself, causing you to question who you are outside of motherhood. It's scary when we don't know what's next, and it's hard to envision what life will look like going forward.

Some of us might dwell on our past mistakes or wonder if we did enough for our children. Can you trust God with their future, their choices, and their safety?

Remember, it's now their chance to figure out life on their own. It's easy to fear they won't make it without your daily guidance and control, but most of our children will. One of the most challenging parts of parenting is knowing they can create their own lives without us. You did it, and they will, too!

Are you asking yourself if there is, in fact, a "what's next?" No matter who you are or what you've done, there is a future for you, stamped with God's fingerprints. Take courage, your destiny is safe and secure.

Journal Prompt:

Write down everything worrying you and consider how to hand them to Jesus.

Prayer Starter:

Lord, I'm giving my worries to You. Help me to trust You fully and remember that You are faithful in all Your ways...

Day 4

The Loneliness Is Real

Scripture reflection:

Fear not, for I have redeemed you; I have called you by your name; You are Mine. When you pass through the waters, I will be with you; And through the rivers, they shall not overflow you. When you walk through the fire, you shall not be burned, nor shall the flame scorch you. For I am the LORD your God. Isaiah 43:1-3

Being confident of this, that He who began a good work in you will carry it on to completion until the day of Christ Jesus. Philippians 1:6

An Encouraging Thought:

Perhaps you got all prepared for your empty nest. You read books, talked to other moms, and maybe listened to some podcasts. But now that you're actually in it, you realize no one could honestly explain how lonely this season can be, and if you're anything like me, it knocked the wind right out of you.

The constant requests for everything from meals and laundry to borrowing the car or helping with homework have evaporated, and silence overrides everything. But you can look at this differently: you aren't a chauffeur, cook, or personal assistant anymore!

Despite the loneliness, Jesus continues to beckon us closer. He is beginning to define our purpose, reminding us we are never truly alone as He designs new rhythms, routines, and dreams for us even when we can't quite discern those dreams yet.

Take this time to enjoy the peace and rest after years of busyness and the seemingly endless and constant push and pull of mothering. We can believe we've lost something or trade that for realizing God is doing something brand-new. If you let Him, He can transform your loneliness into a time of anticipation and purpose, as Paul says in Philippians 3:13, *forgetting those things which are behind and reaching forward to those things which are ahead.*

Loneliness will continue to hound you if you focus on what's missing instead of what's present. This is your sacred opportunity to begin looking forward.

Goals for Today:

Take some time to focus on what's in your hand right now. Do something for yourself that you never had time to do when the children were home.

Common Obstacle:

The deep sense of isolation as you transition to your empty nest.

Overcoming the Obstacle:

It creeps in quietly, almost unnoticed. You used to be so busy, but now you look at your empty calendar in shock. No more games to attend, no late-night talks with your teenager, far fewer texts than you used to have, and before you know it, isolation takes hold. The enemy whispers that you're alone, forgotten, and no longer needed, tempting you to believe you've reached the end of your purpose. But that's a lie. The truth is you were never meant to do life alone.

God is a God of relationships and connections. He designed us for community and to walk alongside each other, to build each other up, to encourage, sharpen, and strengthen one another. Isolation is never from God. It's a nasty tactic of the enemy to keep us sidelined when God calls us to move forward.

In the solitude, the ghost of the past whispers memories and moments gone but not forgotten, making the emptiness more striking. How do you combat it? Prayer first. Jesus will use your seasons of solitude to draw you closer to Him as He begins refining and revealing your purpose beyond motherhood.

Invest in the relationships around you, your husband, friends, family members, etc. Say yes to invitations. Be the first to reach out to a mom going through the same thing. I realize it's an adjustment, but Jesus is walking with you preparing new opportunities and deeper connections. Loneliness is temporary, but God's presence and power are constant. You are not forgotten, and you are not alone! *God sets the lonely in families.* Psalm 68:6 (NIV)

Think about how your emotions are controlling you right now. How are they affecting your attitude, your health, and energy level? Sometimes, the very thing stopping us is the one we are determined to hold on to. Is it keeping you from spending time with the Lord? Be wary of its power to guide your day. There is nothing wrong in feeling what you're feeling, but ask yourself if these emotions are taking over, and then give them to the Lord and let Him guide you. *Some days, you have to fight for the joy.*

A Journal Prompt:

Think about what the Lord may be saying to encourage your heart. You've given up a lot, but what have you gained in raising your children and sending them on their way?

A Prayer Starter.

Lord, help me to see the enemy's tactics. Help me start looking upward and outward and focus on what is right in front of me...

Day 5

The Gift of More Time

Scripture Reflection:

So teach us to number our days that we may gain a heart of wisdom.
Psalm 90:12

Encouraging Thought:

One of the unexpected gifts of the empty nest is the sudden abundance of time. For years, the needs of others dictated your schedule—school pickups, sports practices, late-night homework sessions, and everything in between. But now, in this gentler and quieter season, you can rediscover the beauty of time and how to use it to refresh your soul and realign your purpose.

Think about it: unless you're going to work, you can wake up in the morning and linger over coffee as you spend time in God's Word without interruption. You can pray with a sense of anticipation listening for His still, small voice as He reveals His plans for this new chapter. If you work, you have more time in the evenings to spend with your spouse or work on projects, go out to dinner, or maybe take a fitness class, for example. This season offers the freedom to enjoy more space in your day, allowing you to explore fresh opportunities and deepen your walk with the Lord in ways that may have felt impossible during the busy years of raising children.

Invest in the activities that bring you joy. Pick up that long-forgotten hobby, try a new skill, or travel to places you've always dreamed of seeing. Spend time with friends who make you laugh, join a Bible study, plant a garden, or volunteer in your community. These are not just "fillers" but chances to thrive, grow, and build new relationships.

If you still have children at home, there will be less pull on your time, giving you a chance to start looking forward to your final empty nest as you begin planning *now* for *then*.

Your marriage can significantly benefit from the gift of more time. You can spend more time with your husband without constantly focusing on your children as you build a deeper connection.

You can use your time not only to refresh your spirit but also to prepare you for the next great adventure He has planned for you. Welcome it!

Goal for Today:

You have more opportunities to linger with the Lord. Make space in your day to spend quiet time reading the Word, journaling your thoughts and prayers, or simply sitting in His presence and listening for His voice.

Common Obstacle:

How to fill the void as you struggle to find purpose or joy in this new season.

Overcoming the Obstacle:

After so many years, the stillness of the empty nest feels like an ache that won't go away. It can bring a deep and unexpected void, one that seems impossible to fill. Your purpose, which was so natural before, now feels unsteady. Joy used to spring up in all the everyday moments but now has grown distant. But the void isn't the end of your purpose, it's the beginning of a new adventure. Discovering joy in your abundance of time will require intentionality, grace, and some practical strategies.

Motherhood has been your ministry and mission field for decades. While your active parenting role has changed, you are nonetheless still called to nurture, influence, and impact others. You are a nurturer and a kingdom builder.

Establish a routine like quiet time in the morning or afternoon or whatever time works best. Get some physical exercise if possible; it helps lower our cortisol levels. Eliminate as many distractions from your life as you can.

You don't have to have everything figured out right now, and it's perfectly okay to have questions. However, as you work through this new phase, avoid overcommitting yourself. Leave some margin in your day so you have the mental and emotional ability to focus on the Lord without feeling overwhelmed.

Pray for the Holy Spirit to guide and sustain you. *He is always there,* even when life is complicated and difficult to understand. As you begin to take these tiny, intentional steps, you will find that time with Jesus helps you sense the richness of your relationship with Him, even when life seems complicated.

Journal Prompt:

Spend intentional time in worship, and write about the dreams, passions, callings, and aspirations you set aside during your parenting years.

Prayer Starter:

Lord, help me realize the value of spending time with You each day. I have fewer obligations now and want to use my time wisely. Show me how to prioritize my spiritual growth over all else...

Day 6
Overcoming Doubt and Anxiety

Scripture Reflection:

I can do all things through Christ who strengthens me. Philippians 4:13

And you shall love the Lord your God with all your heart, with all your soul, with all your mind, and with all your strength. This is the first commandment. Mark 12:30

Encouraging Thought:

How are doubt and anxiety, two of our most potent enemies, doing their best to sabotage your future? You've never been in this place before, and it's frightening, to say the least. All the questions we've discussed–who am I now, am I still relevant, and does God have an after party for me–all come crashing down, causing us to worry and question everything about the empty nest. They creep in and quietly whisper, "What now?"

I questioned everything when my daughter left home to pursue her future. I wondered if my best years were behind me, convinced I was all alone and no one could *possibly* understand what I was going through.

But doubt and anxiety began to fade when I remembered who I belonged to. I knew my identity wasn't only in my role as a mom but in my relationship to Christ. He showed me I was still called, loved, and had a function in His kingdom. He made clear that His plan for me didn't end when my daughter moved out. As I began to trust Him, my doubt ebbed, and my anxiety disappeared.

You don't have to figure out your whole path, just take the next step of faith.

Goal for Today:

With God's help, commit to taking on a task you feel unsure about. Make that phone call, sign up for that course, start that book. Do whatever you've been hesitant to do.

Common Obstacle:

Self-doubt and focusing on your weaknesses and limitations.

Overcoming the Obstacle:

Doubt and anxiety have a sinister way of taking advantage of our weakness as they weasel their way in when life feels overwhelming. They can paralyze us, stopping us from doing anything productive.

Are you questioning your abilities? Are you praying and not receiving the answers you're hoping for? Maybe you're feeling overwhelmed and not sure of anything anymore. I get it. Those thoughts are frustrating to wrestle with. You may be tempted to compare yourself to other moms who seem to have it all together, only causing you to question your beliefs and feel inadequate. Maybe you're doubting God has a plan for you or that you can accomplish what He is calling you to do.

Some of the enemy's favorite lies are, "No one needs you," "Your purpose is over," "You have nothing left to offer," and "Your kids don't need you anymore." But that's not what God says. Yes, you're in a murky place, but God never asks us to travel there alone.

Neither anxiety nor doubting is a sign of weakness or a lack of faith. You're doing your best to seek God and understand the changes happening in and around you.

What will get you through this stage? Prayer and spending time in the Word are my go-to's. Talking it through with your spouse, pastor, women's ministry leader, or a mature Christian friend can bring comfort and sound biblical advice. It's okay to question, we all do it at some point in our journey with God. It's never something to be ashamed of.

Community is critical, especially in the beginning, because we grow stronger when we have others to walk with us. They give us spiritual and emotional support, can encourage us when we're having a tough day, and can connect us with others traveling the same road.

When doubt and anxiety rear their ugly heads, breathe deeply and release them to Jesus. Repeat Philippians 4:13 and imagine God standing beside you, equipping you for the task. *I can do all things through Christ who strengthens me.* Philippians 4:13

Journal Prompt:

Think about your most significant doubt and source of anxiety right now. Journal what it is and what you think is causing it.

Prayer Starter:

Lord, thank You for being my strength. Help me rely on You and trust that with You, I can do anything...

Day 7

The Power in the Possible

Scripture Reflection:

I will instruct you and teach you in the way you should go; I will guide you with My eye. Psalm 32:8

Encouraging Thought:

Sometimes, we simply need to pause, breathe, and allow God to renew our hearts. Renewal isn't a result of striving but of resting in Him. This season is about God drawing your heart into what's possible

You've spent years doing all the mom things. But now, God is inviting you into a fresh chapter. This is your appointed time to rediscover your passions, grow in faith, and embrace the unique purpose God has planned for you.

Is there a dream you've put on hold? Is it a creative pursuit, a new career, or a ministry calling? Maybe this is the season to deepen your relationship with the Lord, to step into mentoring younger women, or to serve in ways you couldn't before.

It's normal to feel unsure or even grieve the life you've known. But take heart: the same God who guided you through motherhood is guiding you now. He has equipped you with all the strength and wisdom you need to face this new stage with courage and grace.

Press into the possibilities right in front of you. Are you leaning in a particular direction? Start exploring it and pray that it's the right direction for you. Nothing is off the table. Ask the mature Christians in your life for counsel and advice. Lean in and know that if it's not God's best for you, He will check you in your spirit.

Research has revealed that women over fifty are the happiest and most fulfilled. This transition may feel challenging, but it's also an invitation to grow, stretch, and experience the abundant life God promises. He has a new future ahead for you, and you can trust Him. There is beauty in this new beginning, and the best is yet to come. Keep your eyes firmly fixed on Him, and step out with faith!

Goal for Today:

Take some time to worship today. Ask God to show you what opportunities He is opening for you in this new season.

Common Obstacle:

Not knowing what your future has in store.

Overcoming the Obstacle:

All the years of focusing on raising children leave many moms unsure about their skills, giftings, or the ability to contribute anything meaningful to the world. The newfound freedom of time can seem empty and overpowering. There are so many potential paths that it's easy to feel paralyzed and unsure where to begin. But your future is ripe with new opportunities, even if you can't see them right now.

What if, instead of fearing the unknown, you embraced the possible? Is it possible that your most significant impact is still ahead of you? Is it possible that God will call you into something new, maybe mentoring, ministry, college, or a brand-new career? Perhaps this season is less about loss and more about growing into the complete woman you were always meant to be.

You are not done, though the enemy would like you to believe it. But God whispers something different. He says, *Behold, I will do a new thing, now it shall spring forth; Shall you not know it?* Isaiah 43:19

Fear of failure can cause us to avoid doing anything at all. Or maybe we're just plain tired. Are you too drained and distracted even to begin wanting to explore what's next? That's perfectly fine, you are under no pressure ... unless you're putting pressure on yourself. Take the time you need. Lean into what God is doing, step forward, and say yes. This isn't the end, this is just the beginning.

Journal Prompt:

Consider where you need renewal and where God may be leading you.

Prayer Starter:

Lord, I know everything is possible with You, but I'm unsure of my next steps or what I should focus on ...

DAY 8

THE CHALLENGE OF CHANGE

Scripture Reflection:

See, I am doing a new thing! Now it springs up; do you not perceive it? I am making a way in the wilderness and streams in the wasteland. Isaiah 43:19

Encouraging Thought:

Change is disconcerting, especially when it descends out of nowhere after years of familiar rhythms and routines. In the beginning, the transition can feel like standing at the edge of a vast, churning sea. You know you have no choice, you have to jump in, but the process of letting go and stepping forward comes with its own challenges.

The empty nest is not an ending; it's a divine transition. Just as trees shed their leaves, preparing for new growth, God asks you to shed the past to make room for what's next.

Ecclesiastes 3:1 reminds us, To everything there is a season, a time for every purpose under heaven. As mentioned in the After Party of the Empty Nest, now is your time to lean into Him, to rediscover the dreams and callings He planted in your heart long ago.

One of the hardest parts is digesting the finality of the transition. The chapter of active, daily parenting has closed, and with it, so much of your identity feels tied to what you've left behind. The loss of purpose and routine is potent.

It's all too easy to focus on our fear and loss of identity. What lies ahead? Will your children be okay without you so close? Will you find fulfillment in this new chapter? These questions can weigh heavily, especially when paired with the bewilderment of your new role.

But as perplexing as this season is, there is hope. God's word reminds us in Isaiah 41:10, *So do not fear, for I am with you; do not be dismayed, for I am your God. I will strengthen you and help you; I will uphold you with my righteous right hand.*

Change *is* hard, but it also provides incredible opportunities. It's your chance to grow, rediscover yourself, and trust God's plan for this new stage. The struggle is real, but so is His faithfulness. You don't walk this path alone, Mama. It will stretch you, but you can decide to grasp hold of the stretching. Step out of the boat of the familiar and walk on water when He calls you.

He loves you too much to leave you where you are, and He's not through with you. Let Him refine you … He loves you unconditionally.

Goal for Today:

Identify one aspect of change in your life and thank God for the opportunities it brings.

Common Obstacle:

Resisting change out of fear or comfort.

Overcoming the Obstacle:

Heavy clouds might obscure your vision right now. The future looks bleak, and you have no grasp on how to let go of all that has defined you for decades.

Many moms feel too emotionally drained to even think about having enough energy to make the effort that change requires. They feel isolated, and the idea of stepping out to forge a new path or form new relationships is daunting.

Life is a series of seasons, each one beautifully designed by the Creator to shape us into His image. But oh, how tender this new season feels. It's bittersweet, isn't it? You've spent years sowing into your children, pouring love, prayers, and wisdom into their lives, and now it's time to let them soar. But preparing your children for adulthood isn't the endgame, *finding the other reason He designed you is the endgame.* You can see it as loneliness and loss of freedom or the gateway to a brand-new future.

It's natural to resist change, but by leaning into God's promises and trusting His plan, you can find the courage to step into your "what's next?" When you're unsure, let this scripture encourage you: *For He Himself has said, "I will never leave you nor forsake you."* Hebrews 13:5

Journal Prompt:

Think about how the Lord has been faithful to you during your active mothering years. Take a few moments to list those times when you saw His faithfulness in action.

Prayer Starter:

Lord, thank You for doing a new thing in my life. Help me to trust You with every change and see Your hand in every new beginning...

Day 9

Trusting God

Scripture Reflection:

And those who know Your name will put their trust in You; For You, Lord, have not forsaken those who seek You. Psalm 9:10

Encouraging Thought:

Each morning is pregnant with grace, ripe with the possibility of catching a glimpse of Jesus, from a leisurely breakfast to a great parking spot, a friend's tears, or a missed opportunity. But we only get enough grace for today. We can't store it up for tomorrow or depend on yesterday's. It's the only grace we have, and if we're not careful, we'll miss *today's* grace.

Every day, Jesus teaches me to abide in grace, reminding me that His yoke is easy and His burden is light. My burdens can weigh me down and fill my heart with guilt. I might be tempted to blame myself for making wrong choices during my childrearing years. But let's be honest, we *all* did because none of us were perfect mothers.

If you listen closely, He will whisper to your heart that *He adores you*, everything about you: the sweet times, the hard days, and the real-life moments. We have daily choices to make about the grace in our lives. We can ignore it or invite it to indwell our hearts. We can deny it or deliver it to others.

We can try to understand it or undertake to know the One who gives it with an open and generous hand. Every day, Jesus teaches us to abide in grace, reminding us that His yoke is easy and His burden light. His grace will go with you as you journey into your future.

The empty nest is not an ending, it's a divine transition. As leaves fall, preparing for new growth, God asks you to release the past to make room for what's next. Even when the path is unclear, He promises to guide you. Take heart, Mama. The nest may be empty, but your heart can be full of His grace, joy, and the promise of beautiful new beginnings. Trusting God means surrendering control and believing He knows best.

Goal for Today:

Consider one area of your life where you are experiencing God's grace.

Common Obstacle:

Struggling to let go of control.

Overcoming the Obstacle:

Maybe you're like me. You schedule your day, write your lists, mark out the details, and get entirely derailed when something messes up your perfect plan, forcing you to change.

Despite the struggle, God loves to take me on what I call ninety-degree turns. Life is going along just fine, and then He comes along and shifts everything in another direction. But, along with the shifts, He's teaching me a lesson: He is in my future, and He's making a way for me before I get there.

He prepares a table before us, He lines everything up, and settles all the details. But it's easy to forget He's already there and to forget He goes before us. We forget that Jesus knows all of our days, each one written with care and purpose.

We see only clouds and mist, but He's the sun shining clear and steady above us. We see stones to make us stumble, but He is the bright morning star navigating our way. He directs our way because *He's already prepared it*. He has leveled the ground to make straight paths for our feet.

He loves you with an everlasting love, and He knows the plans He has for each and every one of you. He's in the here and now, and He's in your future, saturating every moment with His presence. You don't need to know what tomorrow may bring, only that He is in each of your tomorrows.

Our job is to simply catch up, one day at a time.

Today, as you meditate on our daily scripture, speak it aloud throughout the day. Picture yourself handing all your plans, worries, and concerns to God in prayer.

Journal Prompt:

Write about that area of your life that feels uncertain or challenging to surrender.

Prayer Starter:

Lord, help me to trust You with my whole heart. Teach me to lean on You, knowing You are perfectly guiding me ...

Day 10
Prayer Changes Us

Scripture Reflection:

Draw near to God and He will draw near to you. James 4:8

Encouraging Thought:

God doesn't care *when* we pray, but He does care *that* we pray! There's no hard and fast rule saying you must get up early for God to pay attention to you. *Whenever* is perfectly fine with Him because He knows and understands the season you're in, and though it would be wonderful to have oodles of quiet time in the morning, it may not be feasible for every mom.

Consider having worship music play quietly during the day. It creates a peaceful atmosphere of praise and will remind you of His presence. He hears every whispered prayer, even the harried and hurried ones!

Pray whenever you can—making dinner, folding laundry, taking a power walk, and honestly, *whenever.* You don't have to rise with the dawn and have perfect silence, beautiful music, and a lit candle to worship God. He knows. Do it when you can, but do it because wherever you do it, He is with you.

Prayer is serious work. It's how we communicate with the Lord. We talk, and He responds as we take the time to listen.

And that's the key, *taking time*. The more often we speak to Him, the more we'll come to know Him.

He doesn't need us to follow specific patterns or check the boxes of reading the word, going to church, memorizing scripture, etc. Although those practices will help us grow, He wants more. He wants us to pursue His presence; as we do, it will inform every moment of our lives.

Sometimes, God seems so huge we're convinced He doesn't hear our prayers. True, we can never get to the bottom of His love for us, but that doesn't mean we can't know Him better than we do right now. Daily habits of prayer, Bible reading, and worship can only serve to strengthen our faith. *Jesus comes where He's wanted.*

Many moms have their quiet time first thing in the morning, but any time you can get away from distractions will work. Make it your holy sanctuary where you purpose to meet with God regularly. Let reading His word become a priority, and journal what you're learning. If you don't know where to start, countless Bible studies are available online. Or maybe there's a local Bible study you can join.

I hope this beautiful scripture encourages you:

Let us know, let us pursue the knowledge of the LORD. His going forth is established as the morning; He will come to us like the rain, like the latter and former rain to the earth. Hosea 6:3

Goal for Today:

Make it a priority to spend time with the Lord in prayer.

Common Obstacle:

Distractions to prayer and hearing from the Lord.

Overcoming the Obstacle:

Modern life is loaded with distractions that barely existed when I was a full-time mom. We might feel overwhelmed with responsibilities as we rush through our day, neglecting time with the Lord. Household noise, phones, notifications, and social media intrude during prayer time, easily distracting us. Our minds naturally drift to to-do lists, worries, or random thoughts, especially when trying to listen for that still soft voice. If possible, put your phone away or put it on airplane mode.

We all have days when worry or unresolved conflicts cloud our concentration. Bring those worries and concerns to God first. Lay your burdens down before Him. Jesus is the best quiet and peaceful place we can find and the one completely safe space to pour out our hearts.

Sometimes, we simply don't know *what* to pray for. We can pray for anything! There is nothing too small or too large for God to handle. He knows exactly what you need. In fact, *He even hears what you aren't able to say.*

As we pray intentionally, prayer can become a tranquil and focused time to spend with Jesus.

Journal Prompt:

What is the biggest distraction preventing you from daily prayer, and how can you remove it?

Prayer Starter:

Lord, show me the distractions that keep me from spending time with you. Show me how to draw closer to You...

Day 11

Embracing Community

Scripture Reflection:

As each one has received a gift, minister it to one another, as good stewards of the manifold grace of God. 1 Peter 4:10

Encouraging Thought:

Now is the ideal time to begin researching what is in your area and start finding community if you don't already have it. We are created for connection, and stepping into a community is vital for finding joy and direction.

Start by reaching out. It may feel intimidating, but you can take small steps. Join a Bible study, a book club, a group at church, or any place where women gather. As you surround yourself with other women in similar life stages, you may be surprised that they can be a wonderful source of encouragement. These new connections will remind you that you're not alone in navigating the empty nest.

Community also opens the door for service. In chapters 14 and 19 of *The After Party of the Empty Nest*, I shared quite a bit about volunteering and mentoring. Volunteer for a cause you're passionate about, or find a younger mom to mentor.

As you join your life with others, you will not only make a difference, but you'll also discover a renewed sense of purpose. Hebrews 10:24-25 encourages us to *consider how we may spur one another on toward love and good deeds, not giving up meeting together, as some are in the habit of doing, but encouraging one another.* (NIV)

Building community can bring deep healing. As you share your heart with others who understand, you create space for growth. Isolation magnifies feelings of loss, but community offers relationships and hope.

As you pursue relationships with others, you'll see how God uses those relationships to enrich your life and deepen your faith. The friendships you make can become a bedrock of support when life gets hard, as they encourage you to step into your future with confidence.

None of us are meant to walk alone. By embracing community, you'll find the strength to thrive in your empty nest because who you walk with shapes where you go.

Goal for Today:

Think about where and how you can begin to find community that will be a blessing to you.

Common Obstacle:

Feeling hesitant or unsure how to reconnect.

Overcoming the Obstacle:

We all have our people who understand us and share our interests, hopes, and dreams, but it's our responsibility to step out and find them. It's normal to feel unsure about putting yourself out there if you haven't for several years. But you don't have to do this alone. Attend a one-time event or a women's meeting at your church. Maybe there's someone you can meet up with for coffee. Low-pressure environments lower the fear of making a permanent commitment.

Is there a friend who can go with you? A familiar face makes it much easier to confront something brand-new. But if that feels too intimidating, there are loads of online groups to join.

Don't give up. Building community can take time. If at first you don't succeed, try, try again! In a few years, you will look back at this time and realize how rich your life has become because you stepped out and found your people.

Journal Prompt:

Write about your interests outside of motherhood. Journal your fear about stepping out and what you can do to overcome it.

Prayer Starter:

Lord, be with me as I venture out and find my people. Show me where You want me to go to find community. Give me the courage to take the first step...

Day 12

Marriage in a New Season

Scripture Reflection:

But from the beginning of the creation, God 'made them male and female.' 'For this reason, a man shall leave his father and mother and be joined to his wife, and the two shall become one flesh'; so then they are no longer two, but one flesh. Therefore what God has joined together, let not man separate. Mark 10:6-9

Encouraging Thought:

For years, life revolved around taking care of your children. You did all you could to raise them into capable and God-honoring adults. But perhaps your marriage began to run on auto-pilot, squeezed into the margins of all the busy, child-focused days. Then, suddenly, the house is quiet.

In that space where noise and activity reigned, today's stillness causes you to realize: *Who are we—the two of us—now without the kids?* It doesn't mean you don't love your husband, but now you must relearn how to be a wife after years of primarily being a mother. The roles that were easy to define before have shifted. And with the shift, you can feel like strangers living under the same roof.

When you hit the empty nest, what was hidden under the noise is magnified. Brushing past unmet needs, tensions, or emotional disconnection was easier when the kids lived at home. But now, the silence makes us sit up and take notice. Conflicts can emerge, and the lack of distraction can bring buried issues to the forefront that you and your husband must confront and work through for the sake of the marriage.

How long has it been since you genuinely enjoyed each other's company without having the kids as a buffer? Are there lingering wounds that were never addressed or an aching need buried under the demands of parenting?

It's easy to believe that life has to return to how it used to be. Are we meant to step back into the early days of marriage? The truth is that God doesn't call us backward but forward. God designed your marriage to grow and deepen through the years. But now, it's about *reinvesting*.

Some of you are excited to have the house to yourselves and lots more time to spend with your husband. But others may feel like you don't know each other anymore. All those little habits you overlooked when your children were home are now starting to drive you crazy. You may wonder if you still have the bandwidth to pour into your marriage. And do you even want to?

Years of focusing on the kids may have left you both on autopilot. The old conflicts that took a backseat have leaped into the front seat of your marriage. You and your husband will each handle this phase of life differently, which can lead to misunderstanding and emotional distance.

It's too important to let your marriage flatline. Now is the moment to view your relationship in a different light. The distraction (or excuse) of kids has disappeared, and the focus falls on your relationship, spotlighting both the positive and negative that may have taken root when the kids were home. Add to all that the midlife changes that wreak havoc on our bodies, causing unexpected emotional upheavals as hormones rage. Maybe you're dealing with menopause, other health concerns, finances, or worries about your children or job.

Because it's just the two of you, you have time to rekindle the romance that may have dwindled over the years. You can dream new dreams and enjoy uninterrupted conversations. And you're free to discover and pursue your shared goals.

As you knit your hearts to God's divine purpose for your marriage, you'll find freedom to grow spiritually as a couple. God has a future for you, and He also has a plan for you *and* your husband, perhaps something you never thought about.

What a joy to look back at the family you built together! Rejoice in God's faithfulness through every phase of your parenting journey, and take pride in the children you raised. Fewer distractions mean more time to focus on emotional and physical intimacy. Remember, you are more than roommates.

Goal for Today:

Take an honest look at your relationship with your husband and evaluate the positive and negative aspects.

Common Obstacle:

Relearning love.

Overcoming the Obstacle:

When we surrender our marriages to God and seek to embrace what *could be*, we begin to see that the empty nest is not an ending but an invitation. An invitation to love deeper, dream bigger, and build something even stronger than before. Marriage is never meant to be defined solely by your years of raising children. It's intended to reflect Christ's love as it grows, endures, and overflows with grace through every season of life.

So, Mama, take heart if you feel the distance and are uncertain about what comes next. God is not finished with your marriage, and He is still writing your story. And this next chapter? It may be the most beautiful one yet.

Behold, I am doing a new thing; now it springs forth, do you not perceive it? Isaiah 43:19

Communicate openly and honestly with your spouse. You are both facing a significant life change that affects him, too, but differently than it affects you. Listen actively when he's speaking, it creates a safe place for him to share. What brought you together in the beginning? Can you revisit what you both used to enjoy doing together?

Maybe there are new goals you can set. Brainstorm about what you envision your future together to look like. Do you have a bucket list of your dreams and goals? Consider what you used to do before raising children took over your life. What did you do for fun?

Marriage is hard work, but your marriage is worth fighting for. None of us want to let yesterday steal what God has planned for tomorrow. Whatever your history with your husband, it doesn't have to limit God's plans for your future. This next chapter might be the most beautiful one yet.

Journal Prompt:

Reflect on your marriage. What's working, and what needs work?

Prayer Starter:

Lord, you put us together. Help me see what obstacles may be getting between us and show me what I can do to strengthen our marriage and honor my husband…

Day 13

When Worry Overwhelms

Scripture Reflection:

And we know that all things work together for good to those who love God, to those who are the called according to His purpose. Romans 8:28

Encouraging Thought:

As unexpected negative byproducts of the empty nest, worries are powerful, and their lies can quickly consume our peace as we wrestle with uncertainty about our abilities, talents, intellect, and more. When we look around, particularly on social media, comparison rears its ugly head, and worry about the future creeps in.

You might be convinced that all your empty nest friends have it all together. They know exactly what path they should follow now that they have more freedom to explore their future. The primary thought swirling through your head is, "Are my best years behind me?" But the truth is, God is never finished with your purpose, it's simply unfolding in a new way.

Your worth is not based on what you do but on who you are in Christ. As Psalm 139:4 so beautifully says, *I will praise You, for I am fearfully and wonderfully made; Marvelous are Your works, and that my soul knows very well.*

Worry whispers ugly lies like these: you're not qualified, you're not good enough, you're forgotten, you're finished. But what does God say? He declares these truths about you: You are chosen, called, and an essential part of His divine plan.

There's a positive aspect as we wrestle with worry. It can strengthen our faith as we realize we *can't* do it alone, we *must* have the Lord help us take our next step. But at times, our emotions lead our decisions. Take them to Jesus and let *Him* guide you. He alone determines your gifts, talents, abilities, and path. He has already chosen your future and purpose, and even though you may have trouble recognizing it right now, He has every single worry and doubt firmly in hand.

Uncovering our future as we battle worry can seem daunting as we struggle with our fear of the unknown. None of us are expected to be perfect. God only requires that we be faithful.

Goal for Today:

Examine your worries, and hand them to the Lord when you pray.

Common Obstacle:

Uncertainty and concern about your future.

Overcoming the Obstacle:

Your purpose isn't gone, but it *has* shifted. Step out in small ways as you sense God leading you in a new direction. If you aren't sensing His leading right now, remind yourself that His timing is perfect, and He will guide you when the time is right.

Can you start a new passion project or join a ministry and volunteer? What about taking a class about something you've always wanted to learn or join a small group? Do something to replace the lies with the truth. You are deeply loved, wildly valuable, and perfectly purposed for this season.

Journal Prompt:

Write about your worries. Then, take a minute to list the unique qualities and gifts God has given *you*. Jesus has a place for all of us in His divine plan! As you look for His fingerprints, you will begin to see where He is working in your life.

Prayer Starter:

Lord, I know You have plans for me, even though I'm unsure where they might take me. Help me to stay faithful even as I grapple with worry...

Day 14

Gratitude

Scripture Reflection:

In everything give thanks; for this is the will of God in Christ Jesus for you. 1 Thessalonians 5:18

Encouraging Thought:

Scripture tells us to give thanks for everything. What's the everything you're struggling with right now? He will never ask us to give thanks for what He has not allowed. Honestly, this might be the hardest lesson I've learned as I've walked with the Lord. Through infertility, a nasty bout with anxiety, a weird season of seizures that hit out of nowhere, and even in the darkest and most painful times, I've learned the hard way to give thanks continually.

How can we give thanks when life gives us heartbreak and loss? But how can we not accept what comes from His hand? He will never tell us to do something He knows we cannot do. I've learned that if Jesus has assigned it to me, it's for my good, however devastating and difficult it may be.

When I went through my season of infertility after an ectopic pregnancy, I was furious at God. He wasn't giving me the one thing I desperately wanted—another baby. All I could see was what I *didn't* have, blinded to all the blessings right in front of me. I'm ashamed to admit how long it took me to realize how completely ungrateful I was for the life He'd given me—a wonderful husband, a beautiful daughter, great friends, and more, *much* more. After years of holding God hostage for not living up to my expectations, I finally saw the beauty of all He'd given me.

It's been a few decades since then, and I realize time gives a perspective you may not have right now. It's hard to be grateful for the unanswered question causing you grief, but as time passes, you'll get a glimpse of God's purpose for your pain. It's easy to get stuck in the past and only see what's missing, ignoring what is in your hand *right now.*

Gratitude shifts our focus from what we don't have to all the blessings everywhere around us. Even in hard times, there is always something to be thankful for.

A heart of gratitude shifts our focus from what's missing to what we already have. What are you most grateful for?

Goal for Today:

Write down five things you're grateful for today and reflect on God's goodness.

Common Obstacle:

Focusing on what feels missing rather than what you have.

Overcoming the Obstacle:

How can we fight for a thankful heart? Look back on your years with your children for the precious gift of raising them. What prayers did He answer for them when they lived with you?

Instead of mourning what you've lost, celebrate what's new. Thank God for your children's independence and maturity.

Thank Him for bringing them into their next phase, whether college, a career, or marriage. Hopefully, you achieved your goal of raising them to be confident, independent men and women who are strong in the Lord. Thank Him for a job well done.

Thank Him for who you are becoming and for new opportunities at your doorstep. He is shaping you into the woman He's called you to be, and you're called to be a world-changer.

Journal Prompt:

Take time today to write honestly about your frustrations and your trouble thanking God for today.

Prayer Starter:

Lord, I'm doing my best to develop a heart of gratitude, but some areas are hard...

Day 15

It's All in the Timing

Scripture Reflection:

The LORD is good to those who wait for Him, to the soul who seeks Him. It is good that one should hope and wait quietly for the salvation of the LORD. Lamentations 3:25-26

Encouraging Thought:

God doesn't always do what we want Him to do when we want Him to do it. We expect Him to answer our prayers with the answer we want, even if it's not the answer we need. We have trouble understanding why He isn't moving or taking away our struggle or pain. Does He even hear us?

What mountain are you dealing with right now? A mountain that simply won't move no matter what you do? A mountain causing you to doubt His grace is real? There's a good reason for your mountain. If you're staring at a mountain that won't move, will you let it mature and teach you? Will you let it draw you closer to the Savior who loves you and knows you better than you know yourself? It takes faith to see God's promises, not wishful thinking, come to pass.

God's timing is perfect, even when it doesn't align with ours. He is in no hurry, at least not in my life. I can look back now and understand how His timing has always made sense. If

He'd given me whatever I wanted back then, it would not have benefitted me the way it does today. One thing I know for sure, there is no testimony without a test.

Goal for Today:

Reflect on a time when God's timing proved better than your own.

Common Obstacle:

Impatience during seasons of waiting.

Overcoming the Obstacle:

How do you handle a holdup? How do you handle what can feel like an interminable wait? What do you do when you know you can't do it alone, you *know* you don't know, and the ones who do know are few and far between?

How do you continue to trust when you're doing the task you're confident you're called to do yet feel stuck in the frustrating place of needing help to finally finish? We know and trust God's timing, but as the days click by, it gets easier and easier to lean on our own understanding.

Have you ever been in a holdup season? We can catapult into worry and self-pity in the wink of an eye. But I know beyond the shadow of a doubt that Jesus does have it all figured out, even when I don't. The only remedy I've found is to pray for patience, surrender my timeline to God, and trust His perfect wisdom.

I need to remind myself daily that it's not in my hands. God's timing is *not* my timing. I know He knows, and I know He's in control, and my job is to drop my constant need for control into His steady hands.

If you're in a waiting and wearying season, run to Him. He's the only one who sees behind the scenes, and He alone knows the timing. Hang in there!

Journal Prompt:

How has God shown His faithfulness to you in the past? How does trusting His timing bring peace?

Prayer Starter:

Lord, help me to trust Your perfect timing in all things. I don't understand the delay, but I know You have wise reasons...

DAY. 16

CONTENTMENT IN CHRIST

Scripture Reflection:

Come to me, all you who are weary and burdened, and I will give you rest. Matthew 11:28

The LORD is my shepherd; I shall not want. He makes me to lie down in green pastures; He leads me beside the still waters. He restores my soul. Psalm 23:1-3

Encouraging Thought:

Over the past four decades, there have been many seasons of walking with the Lord when I didn't believe He was enough. I believed a lie, and it was a simple one. If I was "good," God was obligated to give me my heart's desire. If He were a good Father, He would give me what I wanted. But in my immaturity, He taught me some powerful lessons.

He isn't interested in my happiness as much as my highest good. No one knows me better than Him, and no one else knows exactly what I need exactly when I need it. My job, our job, is to trust Him even when we don't understand and even when we don't like it. It's the tricky but oh-so-necessary part of finding contentment in Christ.

Anything in life I think can satisfy more than Jesus simply won't. He will have nothing less than my whole heart, full of Him and empty of all else, including every idol rattling around I feel compelled to bow down to. The good things we desire, like children, finding a spouse, or the perfect job, can all become idols if we let them.

Mama, nothing you desire—not the relationship, not the job, the raise, the position, the spouse, the influence or recognition, the income, the platform–none of it compares to one real moment in God's presence. As John Piper famously says, *"God is most glorified in us when we are most satisfied in Him."*

And God is most glorified when He can look into our hearts and see His face reflected there because our hearts are so full of *Him*.

Goal for Today:

Take a good look at your beliefs about God and see whether they fit with the truth.

Common Obstacle:

Believing God owes you something.

Overcoming the Obstacle:

Take it from one who's been there and done that. The best thing we will ever have is Jesus. Whatever good thing you want, no matter how good it seems right now, can't ever compare to what He has in store. He's so much more than we think, and He alone knows exactly what's best for us. Let Him peel back the layers and get to your heart. It's part of the maturing process.

You will gain intimacy and contentment with Him as you allow Him access to your deepest desires and submit to His profound lessons. As He takes you through and you find He *comes through,* as you gain firsthand knowledge of His faithfulness, you'll hear His heartbeat, and He will send you out to bring comfort, healing, and hope to others. Don't be afraid to trust Him with your "Why, God?"

Journal Prompt:

Take an honest look at your life and write about where you might lack contentment.

Prayer Starter:

Lord, forgive me for thinking You owe me anything. I owe You my life, and I desire to find contentment in You alone ...

Day 17

God is in Your Future.

Scripture Reflection:

Your eyes saw my substance, being yet unformed. And in Your book, they all were written, the days fashioned for me, when as yet there were none of them. Psalm 139:16

Encouraging Thought:

He orders our steps every day. I mistakenly believe I have to control everything and make it happen a certain way. Until He reminds me that:

- I'm not in charge.
- He sees the end from the beginning.
- He's already written all my days in His book.
- He cares about my future even more than I do.

Imagine what it would look like to so wholly trust Jesus that we never doubted or second-guessed Him or lost faith.

I think I know what it would look like. It would look like peace. I believe it would look like faith, and I'm convinced it would look like trust.

Jesus trusted God all the way to death on the cross and back again. He went, He rose, and He will return. He wants us to live like Him, follow Him, find the narrow path, and stick to it. He knows the way because He's already lived it.

Goal for Today:

Identify one negative thought and replace it with a truth from scripture.

Common Obstacle:

Forgetting He knows the end from the beginning.

Overcoming the Obstacle:

Jesus knows the way and goes before us, setting everything up and making a path for our feet before we ever get there. He's preparing a table for us, putting everything in order, lining it up, and putting all the details perfectly in place because God is in our future. He orders our steps even when we have fallen on our faces.

You might believe nothing is happening because day after day, it's the same. You want to think there's more but can't sense any change. But just because you can't see change doesn't make it any less real. Just because you can't hear doesn't mean it's silent. Just because you can't feel them doesn't mean arms of love aren't wrapped tightly around you. And just because you can't taste doesn't mean the banquet's not being spread.

Right now, a significant shift has taken place, and life feels strange and out of order, churning and changing at the same time, and we pour out our hearts to Him like He doesn't already know each and every one of the challenges we're experiencing.

He cares deeply about your hopes and dreams, desires, wants, and prayers. You might not be able to see what He's doing behind the scenes, but He's working on your behalf, putting all your ducks in a row.

Believe in your future, Mama. Take God at His word and trust He has a good plan for you. Thank Him for what you have, and know He is with you. His plan may look different than yours, but you *can* trust Him. Make every effort to get to know Him *now* before the season changes again. Take the time to get low and quiet, it's the best way to hear His heartbeat. When you do, you will find He truly is enough.

Journal Prompt:

Share your frustrations, what is bothering you, what are you worrying about, and what is scaring you.

Prayer Starter:

Lord, You know the way I take, and You go before me. Help me trust in that truth and give my future to You...

DAY 18
SEEKING JOY

Scripture Reflection:

"Sing, O barren, you who have not borne! Break forth into singing, and cry aloud, you who have not labored with child! For more are the children of the desolate Than the children of the married woman," says the LORD. *"Enlarge the place of your tent, and let them stretch out the curtains of your dwellings; Do not spare; Lengthen your cords and strengthen your stakes. For you shall expand to the right and to the left, and your descendants will inherit the nations, and make the desolate cities inhabited. "Do not fear, for you will not be ashamed;* Isaiah 54:1-4

Encouraging Thought:

I don't know about you, but I never felt like singing during the start of my empty nest. Singing didn't seem appropriate. But if we're willing to sing in the difficult season, just watch what God does.

Sing in this Isaiah passage of scripture means "to give a ringing cry of joy and exultation." Sing before your circumstances change. Sing in the barren season when it looks like all hope is lost, the sky is gray, the earth is hard, and no seed has any shred of hope for life.

Sing into the dark and watch the light spring forth because it will. You WILL expand to the right and the left. You will NOT be ashamed. Let Him gather you and have mercy on you. He sees and loves you so!! The days will not always be this dimly lit, the season will change, and hope will again rise up. *Hold tight to the One who's holding you.*

Joy isn't based on circumstances but on God's presence. Joy is a fruit of the Spirit and a gift from God, and it's how we respond when we are aware of His great love for us. It's an eternal perspective, reminding us we are citizens of heaven *first.* The world assures us we can find joy in accolades, money, a makeover, weight loss, a bigger house, fame, fortune, etc. But God's joy is altogether different.

Jesus tells His disciples *Therefore, you now have sorrow; but I will see you again, and your heart will rejoice, and your joy no one will take from you.* John 16:22

Goal for Today:

Find one simple activity that brings you joy today and do it with gratitude to God.

Common Obstacle:

Believing joy is out of reach or dependent on life being "perfect."

Overcoming the Obstacle:

Sometimes, you have to fight for joy. It's the fruit of a life trusting God in every moment, whether heartbreak or hardship.

That's *eternal* joy. It's not the joy the world gives, it's the joy of following Jesus. It's a heart willing to live in obedience knowing He will never, ever leave us or forsake us. Biblical joy is a far cry from temporal joy. That kind of joy comes and goes and wholly depends on our circumstances. True joy comes in knowing that we know Christ and will see Him and live with Him forever.

We can find great joy in community as we spend time with family and friends. We can share our sorrows and pains, hopes and dreams. However discouraging life gets, we can still experience true joy as we lift our circumstances to the Lord, even when they seem beyond our control. Even in our challenges, His joy strengthens and uplifts us.

If the joy of the Lord is our strength, how can we not accept what comes from His hand?

C.S. Lewis says this: *Joy is the serious business of heaven.*

Journal Prompt:

Write about how joy has sustained you in hard times and what you can do to cultivate it in your life today.

Prayer Starter:

Lord, thank You for guiding me into this new season. Help me trust Your plans and find joy and peace in this journey…

Day 19

A New Normal

with Your Children

Scripture Reflection:

I have no greater joy than to hear that my children walk in truth. 3 John 1:4

Encouraging Thought:

It's a massive swing from worry and control to trust and faith. Your relationship with your child has shifted, and you're in the midst of figuring out the best way to honor their independence while staying connected. What boundaries do you need to establish with your now adult children? It's an adjustment, a pivot from the life you knew, and a substantial redirection toward your future and purpose. How you show up in their lives has shifted, but can you show them that *you* are venturing out into new experiences, new relationships, and new passions just like they are?

Your kids are free to experience life on their own with all its ups and downs, scary choices, and exciting moments. How do you find your way through your need to maintain control yet understanding you must let go? The best antidote to worry that I've discovered is prayer. It's the most potent weapon in our arsenal as we battle the natural fear that comes alongside us as we watch our children figure life out on their own.

You aren't responsible to fix every problem and solve every obstacle in your child's life, and you don't have to unravel, repair, or heal anything for them.

No matter what, they know there is one place in the world where they are loved for who they are, without judgment and without reservation. Kids do mess up and they will mess up. That's why I always say parenting is not a spectator sport. It will tax you to the moon and back, drain you, and fill you up all on the same day, sometimes at the same moment.

When our kids are little, they are delighted to snuggle with us. Many mornings, we may wake up with one or more of them in our beds. But then they grow up, desperate to be a separate, independent adult.

Until the crisis hits.

The huge blunder is made, the betrayal happens, the loss takes their breath away, and then, well, it all comes back to Mom because she loves them regardless of any mistake they made. The older they get, the fewer and farther between those mom times happen. Treasure those raw and real moments, Mama. Always be that safe place where the tears can fall because, as certain as the sun follows the rain, trust will follow, and your love will heal.

Goal for Today:

Giving your worries, fears, and need to control to Jesus.

Common Obstacle:

The need to stay in control and fix every problem.

Overcoming the Obstacle:

You and your children are facing new challenges and changes that can feel strange and difficult to avoid. Let them see you dealing with your *own* issues and figuring them out. I've said for years that your children will follow what you model. So, model strength and confidence, courage and conviction. Let them see you diving into your new purpose and path. *Your* confidence will give *them* confidence to figure out their complex questions about life.

They are watching how you handle life now that they're gone. As they see you move into new opportunities and purposes, they will have more confidence to move into their own. They don't need guilt thrust upon them because Mom is heartbroken that they have moved on. Let them see you thriving, not just surviving.

In the secret place, the place they don't see, the sacred place of prayer, continue to fight for their future and their destiny. I take God at His word, and I fight the good fight of faith, the fight of belief. And I stand my ground. They may be out of your house, but they are never out of your heart.

The weapons of my warfare? Love. Because that's how we mamas do it.

Journal Prompt:

Write about what you're doing to show your kids that you're handling the empty nest now that they are out of the house.

Prayer Starter:

Lord, I want to give my child space and freedom to move into the life You have for them. Help me understand my new role as I put them in Your hands.

DAY 20

SERVING OTHERS

Scripture Reflection:

Jesus, knowing that the Father had given all things into his hands, and that he had come from God and was going back to God, rose from supper. He laid aside his outer garments, and taking a towel, tied it around his waist. Then he poured water into a basin and began to wash the disciples' feet and to wipe them with the towel that was wrapped around him. John 13:3-5 (ESV)

Encouraging Thought:

If we strive to live like Jesus, servanthood is our touchstone because Jesus is our model. We serve because He showed us the way. When He washed the disciples' feet, He illustrated the humility wrapped around every act of service we do.

Now that you're in your empty nest, you have more time. Even if you have a full-time job, you may now have the bandwidth to give of yourself and your talents. There is no blueprint for serving other than the one Jesus gives us. It can look like anything.

When we serve, we become agents of change as we live out Christ's love day by day. There is nothing too small or too humbling to take on. It's how we show our love to others, and it can give us great joy in the process, along with a deep and fresh sense of purpose and fulfillment.

When we serve, we follow what Jesus taught and show God's love to others. Sometimes, in our serving, we may find the exact purpose we're created for and the next step in our journey with Him. Serving has many faces and many benefits.

Goal for Today:

Find one way to serve someone today, whether through a kind word, an action, or simply being present.

Common Obstacle:

Feeling too busy or unqualified to make a difference.

Overcoming the Obstacle:

There is a massive need all around us, and none of us are unqualified to serve. God has a need only you can fill. Pray for direction and ask Him to show you your role. It may be volunteering, financially supporting someone in need, mentoring, or doing random acts of kindness in your neighborhood. Do you have an elderly neighbor or new mom living near you? Are there practical ways to serve her? Serving has many faces; even with a busy life, there are always places to give.

When we go out to dinner, my husband and I love to ask our server how we can pray for them. We do it when they bring us our check, usually putting our hands on theirs. No one ever says no when we ask if we can pray for them. It's a small act, but the results have been beautiful to watch. Some servers have simple needs, but others are far more profound, like the single mom with a sick child who didn't know how she would be able to both work and be with her child at the same time. Or the young man scared to leave for college or the new believer who needed encouragement. We have had so many powerful encounters simply by offering to pray.

There are a million and one ways to serve. As you pray, God will give you a sense of where He wants to use you to serve others. Remember that God values small acts done with great love. Start with what's within your reach.

Journal Prompt:

Who could use encouragement or support today, and how can you serve them in a meaningful way?

Prayer Starter:

Lord, give me a servant's heart today. Show me how and where I can share Your love through acts of kindness and humility...

DAY 21
DREAMING WITH GOD

Scripture Reflection:

For assuredly, I say to you, if you have faith as a mustard seed, you will say to this mountain, 'Move from here to there,' and it will move; and nothing will be impossible for you. Matthew 17:20

Have I not commanded you? Be strong and of good courage; do not be afraid, nor be dismayed, for the LORD your God is with you wherever you go. Joshua 1:9

Encouraging Thought:

"Go big or go home!" We've all heard that expression, but the truth is that most of us won't go big. We've forgotten *how* to dream big for ourselves and we don't dream big for anyone else. We tend to let life happen and allow the daily drudgery to put a stop to dreaming, no longer imagining what the future may hold. We think, when I see it, I'll believe it when the truth is, *when we believe it, then we'll see it* when we're willing to *call into being things that were not.* Romans 4:17 (NIV)

All vision, all accomplishment, all dreams begin with listening to that still, small voice saying, "*What if….*"What *if* you wrote that book? What *if* you took that mission trip? What *if* you started that company? What *if* you went back to school? What *if* you lost the weight? What *if* you stepped out of your comfort zone and began that ministry haunting you since high school?

We all have those holy tugs, something just on the edge of what's possible, a pursuit worth having but one with a price attached. The price? Time. Work. Sweat. Sacrifice.

God will drop the "what ifs" in our spirit from time to time. True dreamers actually think about it and start believing that maybe God has something there. "Maybe I *can*."

Ten years ago, I never dreamed I'd write a book. For heaven's sake, it never even entered my mind. But when God dropped a little "what if" in my heart, I didn't reason it away but found myself thinking about it. The more I thought about it, the more I realized *He had already written the book in my heart and life.* All I had to do was dig down and pull it out. Yes, it involved time and sacrifice, missed lunches, and shopping trips with friends. But God handed me a gift that will hopefully keep giving and inspiring.

What about you? I know you have a "what if." We all do. Let me encourage you today…step out! Take the risk, dare to dream. Someone's going to change the world, and it might as well be you. After all, you are *fearfully and wonderfully made!*

Goal for Today:

Take some time to throw caution to the wind and imagine what you could be if you had no restrictions and could be anything you want.

Common Obstacle:

Getting out of your own way.

Overcoming the Obstacle:

If you've convinced yourself God can't use you, let me gently remind you of something: that's not His voice speaking—it's the enemy's. God specializes in doing extraordinary things through the most unlikely people with the most ordinary lives. But here's the truth, Mama: you've got to get out of your own way.

It starts with surrender, laying down the doubts, insecurities, and every excuse you've carried for far too long. "I'm too old." "I've made too many mistakes." "It's too late." Those thoughts are lies the enemy has designed to keep you stuck. But God's truth says, *My grace is sufficient for you, for My strength is made perfect in weakness* (2 Corinthians 12:9).

He's not waiting for you to be perfect. He's waiting for you to say yes.

Get quiet before Him and ask, *"Lord, what's my next step?"* Don't overcomplicate it. It can be big or small, like reaching out to someone who needs encouragement, dusting off an old dream, or stepping into a new ministry. You don't need a grand plan, you simply need to listen and consider it in the moment.

And trust me, if He's stirring something in your heart, He will equip you. He's not interested in your resume, He's interested in your availability. I'm sure you've heard this saying: God doesn't call the qualified, He qualifies the called. It's true! Because if God calls you to it, He will equip you to do it.

When you get into the Word, you can begin to replace every lie you believe about yourself with God's truth. Make an effort to surround yourself with people who will remind you *who you are in Christ*. And then, step out, even if it feels shaky at first.

What's your "and also" as in, I'm a mom "and also ____" (fill in the blank)?

God is always on the lookout for impossible dreamers, the ones who'll take a tiny seed of belief, plant it deep in the soil of faith and carefully tend it as it grows.

If you're faithful in this, what He whispers to your heart today will one day be shouted to the world. God has a plan for your life that goes beyond what you can imagine. You don't want to miss it because you were too afraid to believe He meant it for *you*. Say yes. Stop holding yourself back … and watch what God can do.

Journal Prompt:

Write down what you believe may be hindering you from stepping into God's dream. How can you surrender control and trust the process?

Prayer Starter:

Lord, it's hard for me to believe You have a dream for me, but I doubt myself, and I doubt You. Show me where I'm getting in my own way…

Day 22

Growth in the Struggle

Scripture Reflection:

Be anxious for nothing, but in everything by prayer and supplication, with thanksgiving, let your requests be made known to God; and the peace of God, which surpasses all understanding, will guard your hearts and minds through Christ Jesus. Philippians 4:6-7

Encouraging Thought:

If you can see it, it's not faith. That's just the way it works. In fact, our common sense will completely contradict the still, small voice, the voice you try to brush away but won't let you sleep. The voice that makes you think, that's *crazy*. That *can't* be what God means.

Yes, it can. The direction, the divine detail, or the idea that doesn't make any sense or that's simply too big for you to get your brain around could very likely be God speaking to your spirit. Especially when it doesn't go away no matter how much you pray.

I believe God has unique dreams, ideas, visions, and concepts that He's just waiting to drop on someone. But He wants us to see it with our spiritual eyes, not our intellect. It's the evidence of things *not seen*... like a shadow that will put substance to your prayer and belief. For me, it usually starts as a glimpse, an inkling, or a subtle passing thought that my common sense urges me to ignore, like writing books when I had no desire to be a writer.

Faith is *un*common, and God's peace is not like the fickle and fleeting calm the world offers. It's a deep, abiding assurance that He is in control, even amid uncertainty.

Goal for Today:

Identify one worry or fear and surrender it to God in exchange for His peace.

Common Obstacle:

Letting uncertainty about the future snatch your peace.

Overcoming the Obstacle:

Surrender. That's one of the scariest words I know. But our surrender is in the exhale. In Jesus' last breath, the ultimate surrender was in His final exhale: *It is finished.*

What do you need to exhale?

When our foundation is secure, we know we're loved, and all is going well, it's easy to believe in our future and feel safe in who we are. But when our foundation cracks and our footing is unsure, it's a short slide into unbelief. Life confuses and confounds us as lying voices echo in our heads, threatening to break us.

We see ourselves earth-bound, weighted down with insurmountable problems. But Jesus sees us above, sitting with Him, resting and at peace.

Some of us may battle depression, fear, anxiety, guilt, and rejection. I've battled all five because I've invited my past to determine my future, forgetting His will for me is blessing, abundant life, and victory.

Our mind is our battlefield, and the only way to change it is by renewing it. In fact, Paul says we are *transformed* when we renew our minds. It's time to change our mindset from fear to faith and stop letting the pain of the past and the fear of the future affect all the potential of the present. We need a new, fresh, godly perspective.

Pray today's scripture, Philippians 4:6-7, asking God to replace your anxiety with His peace:

Be anxious for nothing, but in everything by prayer and supplication, with thanksgiving, let your requests be made known to God; and the peace of God, which surpasses all understanding, will guard your hearts and minds through Christ Jesus.

Journal Prompt:

What do you need to exhale today?

Prayer Starter:

Lord, thank You for the gift of Your peace. Help me to surrender my worries to You, knowing You are in control…

Day 23
Steps to Intimacy

Scripture Reflection:

Call to Me, and I will answer you, and show you great and mighty things, which you do not know. Jeremiah 33:3

The LORD your God in your midst, the Mighty One, will save; He will rejoice over you with gladness, He will quiet you with His love, He will rejoice over you with singing. Zephaniah 3:17

Encouraging Thought:

How do we get close to Jesus? The word "intimacy" is tossed around as if we all understand what it is and how to achieve it. However, as in marriage, intimacy is developed over time.

How do you know if you have intimacy with God? You'll know if you have a peace and contentment you can't explain, drawing you to spend more time with Him. Intimacy is the desire to follow His will, even when it's hard to understand. As you spend time with Jesus, you know He accepts and loves you, imperfections and all. Our faith grows as we experience His love and forgiveness. Intimacy with Jesus is like a garden, it will only grow if you tend it.

These steps may help you as you pursue intimacy with Jesus.

- **Prayer.** Have a conversation with Him. Tell Him your deepest desires, sorrows, hopes, and dreams. Praise Him, thank Him, and ask Him for what you need. When we draw near to Him, He will draw near to us. Prayer is a conversation. We talk, and He responds as we take time to listen. The more often we speak to Him in prayer, the better we'll be able to know Him and hear Him.

- **Journaling.** It's an eye-opening practice to see the many ways He has been faithful to us. We can journal our questions, thoughts, frustrations, answers to prayer, scriptures, and anything that may impact us in that moment. I love to look back at answered prayers from past years and gratefully reflect on how He is working and moving in my life.

- **Spend time with Him.** That's the only way to become intimate with anyone. Take time to sit quietly away from all distractions, read His word, meditate (think about) what you're reading, and ask Him to clarify it if you don't understand it. Daily time with Jesus will rejuvenate your spirit.

- **Quiet time.** Make it the most important thing you do each day, and find a peaceful place to have it. Many women have quiet time first thing in the morning, but any time you can get away from distractions will work. It might be while you're in your bedroom or front porch, in your car for a few minutes before you go to work, etc. Make it your holy sanctuary where you purpose to meet with God regularly. Read His Word and take a few minutes to journal if possible. Journaling doesn't have to be long, profound, or complicated. A few words, sentences, or scriptures will do.

As we pursue intimacy, we will gain more and more wisdom. King Solomon chose wisdom over every other earthly thing, including wealth, longevity, and power over his enemies.

God not only gave him wisdom, but He gave him all the other blessings as well.

Goal for Today:

Figure out where and when you can have your daily quiet time.

Common Obstacle

There are so many obstacles to intimacy to discuss, so we'll focus on one: bitterness.

Overcoming the Obstacle:

Here we sit in an empty house, utterly distracted by the hurt of this season. We don't deserve this, we think, or this is too hard, or if God is so good, why am I so miserable? When we focus on the hard parts of the empty nest and how we've been wounded or wronged, it blinds us to God's grace and His love for us.

Some of you may be dealing with devastating circumstances, but intimacy with Jesus can bring healing even in the toughest times. The antidote to bitterness is love, and as we take time away with the Lord, we will find His peace saturating every moment of our lives.

Maybe you try to make the time to pray, but you feel like your prayers are bouncing off the ceiling, and you're distracted by everything on your to-do list. You don't know if Jesus even hears you. But you know you need His grace and strength to get through the challenges of your empty nest.

Fellowship with other believers can help tremendously on your journey. It encourages me to remain faithful as I see a friend's prayers answered, even if mine haven't been. I know He answers *every* prayer in His perfect timing.

Part of faith is trusting that He hears us and that our prayers are important to Him. It takes time and effort to develop a deep relationship with Jesus. But as you read your Bible, pray, and journal, He will begin to reveal Himself to you in deeply personal ways.

Journal Prompt:

Pour your frustrations on the page and tell Him what's bothering you. Be transparent and ask Him to show Himself to you today.

.

Prayer Starter:

Lord, I'm frustrated with where I'm at and how I'm feeling. I know that my relationship with You needs to grow. Show me Your love and how I can begin to know You more deeply…

DAY 24
FINDING CONTENTMENT

Scripture Reflection:

Rejoice always, pray without ceasing, in everything give thanks; for this is the will of God in Christ Jesus for you. 1 Thessalonians 5:16-18

Encouraging Thought:

Contentment during trials—it feels almost impossible, doesn't it? How can we be content when we're depressed, our dreams are delayed, or our prayers seem to go unanswered? The truth is contentment isn't about perfect circumstances, it's about trusting God in the middle of the difficult ones.

I've learned this the hard way. I've faced broken dreams, seasons of waiting, and heart-wrenching disappointments. Each time, I had a choice: let frustration and fear take over or lean into God's faithfulness. *Contentment is a choice*—a daily surrender to trust that God is still good even when life isn't.

The Apostle Paul said it best: *for I have learned in whatever state I am, to be content* Philippians 4:11. Paul wasn't content because everything was moving smoothly. Quite the opposite, in fact. He was content because He knew the One who held his life in His hands. His contentment came not from his circumstances but from confidence in God's sovereignty and faithfulness.

When we choose to trust Jesus in the trial, to thank Him even when life looks bleak, something powerful happens. A deep faith and a quiet heart begin to grow, and we stop striving for the answers and rest in His presence. *He is enough*, even when nothing else feels like it is.

Contentment doesn't mean we stop praying for breakthroughs or relief. It means we surrender the timing and outcome into His hands, trusting He's working all things for good, even the waiting, even the hardship, and even the heartache of the empty nest.

So, Mama, let go of the striving. We don't find contentment in the absence of trials but in the presence of Jesus. Choose to trust Him right where you are. He has never left your side, and He never will. Let that truth settle deep in your soul, and you'll find peace—right in the middle of the storm.

Goal for Today:

List three blessings in your life right now, and thank God for each one.

Common Obstacle:

Comparison.

Overcoming the Obstacle:

A big obstacle to contentment? *Comparison.*

It sneaks in quietly, stealing joy and planting poisonous seeds of discontent. You're doing great until you scroll through social media or hear about someone else's success. Suddenly, your life feels small, your progress slow, and your blessings less than someone else's. Comparison turns God's gifts into "not enough."

The enemy loves to use comparison because it shifts our focus from God's faithfulness to what we think we're missing. We forget that God's plan for each of us is beautifully unique, perfectly timed, and designed with love. When we measure our lives against someone else's highlight reel, we blind ourselves to the good things God is already doing in our own lives.

So, how do we overcome it?

Contentment begins with gratitude. When you feel that twinge of envy, stop and thank God for what He's already given you. An attitude of thanksgiving rewires your heart to recognize His blessings. Your race is not her race. Your story is not her story. God's not asking you to be like anyone else, He's asking you to trust Him with *your* journey. Make every effort to fix your eyes on Him, not on anyone else in your life.

Jesus is never late, and He's never early. His plans for you are good, even when they unfold differently than you expected. Rest in the truth that He sees you, knows you, and works all things for your good.

When we focus on His faithfulness, comparison will lose its menacing power. And that's when contentment begins to bloom. Trust Him. He's writing a beautiful story *just for you.*

Journal Prompt:

Write about what contentment means to you. How can you
begin to thank God even when life is hard?

Prayer Starter:

Lord, help me to find my contentment in You. Teach me to trust that You are enough and to be thankful for the blessings You've given me...

Day 25

Renewing Strength

Scripture Reflection:

Therefore, whether you eat or drink, or whatever you do, do all to the glory of God. 1 Corinthians 10:31

Encouraging Thought:

Now that your time is your own, without the daily grind of mothering, you have more freedom to take care of yourself. The word "self-care" is tossed around as either the perfect, well-deserved antidote to a stress-laden life, or it's viewed as selfish and self-focused, desiring to put your needs above others. We can become so self-focused we neglect God's call. But is it?

Self-care can be complex for Christian women. We see it in one of two ways: as a necessary way to steward our lives, health, and strength or as a self-indulgent distraction from our true purpose.

Stewarding our health is biblical. 1 Corinthians 6:19-20 tells us, *Or do you not know that your body is the temple of the Holy Spirit who is in you, whom you have from God, and you are not your own? For you were bought at a price; therefore glorify God in your body and in your spirit, which are God's.*

When we prioritize rest, good nutrition, and exercise, we can serve our family at our best, with strength, not exhaustion. Jesus modeled rest beautifully. He took time away from the crowds to reconnect with His Father. If Jesus needed to rest, don't you think we do, too?

Here are a few biblical ideas for self-care:

- Time with the Lord
- Exercise
- A healthy diet
- Prioritize sleep
- Limit social media
- Set boundaries
- Find a creative outlet
- Mentor or volunteer
- Open your home for hospitality

And many more you can add.

Goal for Today:

Take a practical step to care for your body and soul, such as walking, eating a healthy meal, or time with a friend.

Common Obstacle:

Feeling too tired or overwhelmed to make changes.

Overcoming the Obstacle:

How do we pour from an empty cup? We risk burnout, exhaustion, and emotional strain. We can invest in our growth in every way without feeling selfish. Self-care strengthens and prepares us for whatever God has for us next.

We can use self-care as an excuse to put our needs ahead of others and exploit a self-focused mindset that distracts us from our greater purpose. But self-care isn't vanity, it's obedience to God's perfect design.

If there is something that both refreshes your soul and gets you ready to serve others, then it's worth doing. You may need to reevaluate it if it distracts you from God's purpose. Self-care can be a righteous way to give you strength and the energy to honor God with your body, mind, and spirit during your empty nest season.

Journal Prompt:

Write about how you can care for yourself in a God-honoring way.

Prayer Starter:

Lord, give me wisdom on how to care for myself mentally, physically, and spiritually today...

DAY 26
STEPPING OUT IN FAITH

Scripture Reflection:

By faith Abraham obeyed when he was called to go out to the place which he would receive as an inheritance. And he went out, not knowing where he was going. Hebrews 11:8

Encouraging Thought:

In *The God Dare*, I wrote how God offers to take us far beyond what we would ever dare to follow. During the beginning of my empty nest, I learned that following God would stretch me, but I had to embrace the stretching and be willing to move forward when He called me.

Stepping out in faith during the empty nest is like standing at the crossroads of what *was* and what *will be*. The kids are gone, your house is quiet, and the question lingers: What's next, Lord?

God is inviting you into something fresh, something that requires faith over fear. But here's the challenge: stepping out in faith is uncomfortable. Some of you may be ready to jump in, you know your next step, and you're eager to get moving. But many of you aren't entirely secure about your future.

The empty nest isn't an ending, *it's an open door.* You won't know every step in advance, but you *will* know the next one.

Pray boldly, dream big, move forward, and say yes. Your obedience in this season will lead to something beautiful, something only God can orchestrate. If you aren't sure what He's calling you to, that's fine, He'll let you know when He's ready.

So take a deep breath, step out with faith, and jump into your new chapter, trusting that the God who led you through motherhood is the same God leading you into your act two.

Goal for Today:

Dig in with God to find out your next steps.

Common Obstacle:

Struggling to define your dream.

Overcoming the Obstacle:

Not every single one of us will know what we are supposed to do the minute our empty nest begins. In fact, most of us won't know. It can be challenging to figure out because you're trying to manage all these strange and unexpected emotions.

You don't have to know right now, but you do want to begin making good use of your time. Some of you might wonder if you even *have* a future or was mothering the only destiny God had for you, and you can't think of one single thing God has gifted you for beyond motherhood.

Please know you have gifts and a future you might have never considered, just like me. I had no idea the plans God had for me. But when He showed me my path, it was up to me to say yes, and when I *did*, He gave me a direction and commitment to jump in with both feet.

What should you do now? During your quiet time, dig in with God. Ask Him to show you where to focus your energy. You're on the threshold of your next chapter, even if you don't know exactly what it is. Your future may be unseen at the moment, but it's beautifully orchestrated by the master Musician. Hold His hand. He will lead you.

Journal Prompt:

How can you begin digging deep with Jesus about your next steps? What do you think they might be?

Prayer Starter:

Lord, I want to believe there is more for my life, but I'm unsure what it could be. I'm doing my best to handle all the emotions swirling through my mind daily. Let Your voice speak louder than mine…

Day 27

Leaving a Family Legacy

Scripture Reflection:

One generation shall praise Your works to another, and shall declare Your mighty acts. Psalm 145:4

Encouraging Thought:

I'm a big believer in the benefit of generations. So often, we think it's only about us and *our* generation. God is laser-focused on us but also on the generations coming after us. How do we gain the big picture, the truth that His plans and purposes are greater than any one individual as they continue from generation to generation?

Leaving a legacy isn't about grand gestures or perfect lives. It's in our daily choices, our steady faith regardless of the circumstances, and the love we plant in our children's hearts. It takes time to leave a legacy, a lifetime, in fact. Even though your children have moved into adulthood, your life speaks louder than your words ever could.

How can you create a legacy that will last? Make faith the foundation of your life. As you walk through the days and years, the highs and lows, let them see you leaning fully on His promises even if specific prayers weren't answered how you'd hoped. Show them your unshakable faith when life shakes you.

You've passed on wisdom during the years you raised your children. They've seen the power of prayer in your example, the answers and miracles that may have changed the trajectory of their lives.

Your words and prayers, unwavering faith, and trust make this the legacy that will echo through the generations to come. That legacy will live on.

Goal for Today:

Trusting that regardless of your past, you can leave your children a powerful legacy of faith.

Common Obstacle

Believing you didn't model faith well enough, and now it's too late.

Overcoming the Obstacle:

Many moms believe their chance to leave a legacy has passed. "I've made too many mistakes. If only I'd prayed more or been more patient. I can't change anything now." Remember, God is not bound by time. As He redeems what was lost, it creates a ripple effect for generations to come. It's never too late for God to use you to leave a legacy of faithfulness to your children.

Joel 2:25 tells us, *I will restore to you the years that the swarming locust has eaten,*

The enemy is patient, and when the time is right, he will worm his way into our minds as he hisses lies of unworthiness and failure. You may believe you're not spiritual enough or strong enough to leave behind any kind of worthwhile legacy. But God doesn't require perfection, only a willing heart. Guilt will paralyze us if we allow it.

As you progress in your journey with Jesus, the transformation others see in you will be a powerful witness, speaking louder than any mistake you may have made. Jesus only asks for our willing hearts because He loves using ordinary moms to do extraordinary exploits. Watch Him work through your small, consistent acts of faith and love.

Leaving a legacy is about who we are becoming in Christ today, not what we've done in the past. God is the author of your story, and He isn't done yet. He sees you according to your destiny, *not* your history. In fact, your legacy is unfolding right now, at this very moment. So step forward with grace! What you leave behind will be more beautiful than you ever imagined.

Journal Prompt:

Take an honest look at your life and write about where you see your legacy beginning to blossom.

Prayer Starter:

Lord, help me understand what legacy I'm leaving behind for my children. Show me where I can make the changes I need to make...

DAY 28
LIVING ON PURPOSE

Scripture Reflection:

Your ears shall hear a word behind you, saying, "This is the way, walk in it," whenever you turn to the right hand or whenever you turn to the left. Isaiah 30:21

Encouraging Thought:

You've arrived at a crossroads, and you can either settle into the background or jump into life as it looks right now. It's your opportunity to live with intention, rediscover the dreams you set aside, invest in your marriage, rekindle friendships, and more.

Living on purpose means you refuse to drift through life, filling the quiet with distractions and busyness that can never fully satisfy you. Instead, it's about seeking God's heart, trusting in His timing, and then saying yes to your next steps. It's the time to step forward, not shrink back.

Purpose isn't so much about striving to prove your worth but waking up each day with a heart willing to say, "Lord, use me." This new phase comes with God's divine invitation to discover the fresh ways Jesus wants to use you. Your life and gifts are needed, valuable, and intended to impact lives.

Remember, your purpose ties you to your Creator, not your role as a mom. Now is the perfect moment to discover who you are in Him. Who were you before motherhood, and how did God shape you during those years? What passions or dreams did you set aside to raise your family? How is He inviting you to grow in this new season?

Your wisdom and experiences are needed and have great value to the world. Think about all the women you can impact, from young moms to newlyweds to other empty nesters. God has given you a story, and your story has power.

All of us have the choice to drift or live on purpose. This new season is an opportunity to discover and walk in the good works He's planned for you.

Goal for Today:

Identify one way to bless someone this week with your gifts or passions.

Common Obstacle:

Drifting

Overcoming the Obstacle:

We drift when we live without intentionality. It's what happens when we let day after day pass without purpose, languish in our pain, and fill our time with distractions instead of direction. Drifting sneaks its way in as one day turns into months, and suddenly, we realize we've been drifting for years, wondering where the time went. We are meant to *live* our days, not merely *fill* them.

It's far too easy to wake up each morning without a plan, letting life happen instead of directing it. Ask yourself: What do you want this season to look like? What does *God* want it to look like? You can passively wait for your future or actively seek it through prayer. God will give you a fresh vision if you ask Him.

You don't need a crystal-clear plan to move ahead. You only need to take your next step. The enemy wants to keep you stuck and hesitant, but action, even small steps, will create momentum that can begin moving you forward.

God didn't create you simply to coast along but to live an abundant life. Ask yourself if the time you spend is drawing you closer to God and your calling. How are you using your gifts to bless others?

The best way to stop drifting is to focus on what truly matters. You haven't been retired, you're being recommissioned into a brand-new calling! So pour into your family, invest time expanding the kingdom, and live each day with eternity in mind, knowing your purpose stretches far beyond yourself.

Journal Prompt:

Write honestly about where you see drift in your life and what you can do to combat it.

Prayer Starter:

Lord, show me where I've been drifting. Remind me of the opportunities You've placed before me as You help me walk boldly into them ...

DAY 29

STEPPING OUT IN FAITH

Scripture Reflection:

Have I not commanded you? Be strong and courageous. Do not be afraid; do not be discouraged, for the LORD *your God will be with you wherever you go.* Joshua 1:9

Encouraging Thought:

I know what it's like to defer a dream, to lay aside your deepest desires, to give and give and give till the memory of your dream fades, becoming nothing more than a shadowy mist. I've laid down what I deeply valued to take up what *He* said is valuable. Because being a mama is one of the most valuable jobs there is.

I raised one child, so I can't relate to all your struggles. My laundry pile was smaller than yours, and I only had one schedule to memorize. I had more free time in my days and more resources to help my daughter define her dream. But here's a truth you can take to the bank:

Mothering well is not about quantity; it's all about quality. Good mothers are good whether they have one child or ten. As you begin to step into your next adventure with Jesus, let me encourage your heart with these truths:

- You can do this.
- You're doing much better than you think.
- You are perfect for the job.
- Some days will be hard.
- Your capacity for joy and sorrow will expand.
- God is with you every second of every day.
- God custom chose you for your children.
- God custom chose your children for you.
- You're not alone. Not for one second.

Courage is not about the absence of fear but His presence in the midst of it. He will equip you with the strength to face any challenge. He is *always* walking with you.

Goal for Today:

Step out in faith and do one thing that you've been avoiding out of fear.

Common Obstacle:

Fear of failure or the unknown.

Overcoming the Obstacle:

Stepping out in faith when you're scared feels like holding on to a bungee cord, unsure if you'll get caught when you jump. Your heart races as doubts flood in. "What if I fail?" "What if I heard God wrong?" "What if I'm not enough?"

Fear often shouts the loudest right before a breakthrough. The enemy would love to keep you paralyzed in that place because he knows what God can do through your obedience.

Faith isn't the absence of fear, it's trusting God more than you trust your fear.

Remember when Peter stepped out of the boat (Matthew 14:29)? He wasn't fearless. The storm was raging, the water was deep, and nothing about stepping out of the boat and into the roaring tempest made any sense. But when he heard Jesus say, *"Come,"* all the storm's chaos melted away, and he stepped out—one shaky foot at a time. And for one exhilarating moment, he walked on water.

You may not be walking on waves, but God calls you to step out in faith. Maybe it's a new ministry, a career change, or starting something that's been in your heart for years. Perhaps it's reaching out to someone or making a decision you've been putting off. It will feel scary and uncertain. But God will meet you right there.

Faith grows when we put a toe in the swirling water before we're ready, trusting God to steady us. He's not asking you to figure it all out. He's asking for your obedience and willingness to trust Him even when the path seems murky.

So, take that step, friend. It's okay if your knees shake and your voice trembles. God delights in your faith, no matter how small it feels. And just like Peter, when your eyes are fixed on Him, you'll find the courage to walk on what once seemed impossible.

Take one step at a time. Jesus will do the rest.

Journal Prompt:

Reflect on a time when you felt God's strength when you were afraid.

Prayer Starter:

Lord, I need Your courage today. Help me trust Your presence and step boldly into Your plans for me...

Day 30

Surrender

Scripture Reflection:

Commit your works to the LORD, and your thoughts will be established.
Proverbs 16:3

Encouraging Thought:

The empty nest is a crossroads. It's a place where the past is familiar, but the future is uncertain. After years of investing in your children, it can be unsettling to ask, "What's next for me, Lord?" But the truth is that this season is not a pause in your purpose—it's your holy invitation to surrender.

Surrender isn't giving up, it's giving over. It's taking every longing, every hope, and every fear and placing them in the hands of the One who has always held your life in His. Maybe you dreamed of a certain kind of relationship with your adult children, and it doesn't look the way you expected. Maybe you feel restless, unsure of what your next chapter should be. Maybe there's a tug to something new, but fear of stepping out pulls you back, making you want to stay safe exactly where you are.

I've not always been good at surrender. I've fought it tooth and nail more often than I'd like to admit. I look at my life and wonder if I'll *ever* reach a higher plane with Jesus. I wonder if

I'll ever be low enough to be good enough. How I want to see myself, who I believe myself to be, is not who I always am.

Surrendering your future to God means releasing *your* plans for *His* purposes. It's trusting that even though you may not know what's ahead, *He does*. It's a good thing we don't have to figure it all out. Jesus knows we don't have a perfect plan, but He asks that we trust Him with our next step. He is still writing your story, one word, one paragraph, and one chapter at a time.

He wastes nothing, Mama. He will use every tear, every holdup, and every experience for His glory.

Your best days are ahead because God's not done with you. So take this moment to step out of the familiar and into an incredible journey with Him. It's time to let go of what was, throw your arms around what is, and trust Him for what's next. Your next chapter is His to write, and He writes the best stories!

Goal for Today:

Write about what God is asking you to surrender.

Common Obstacle:

Forgetting past blessings during current challenges.

Overcoming the Obstacle:

It's not biblical to give up hope. We do it, I do it, but it dishonors who God says He is. Many times, we simply need to surrender and agree to give in and accept God's will, even if it's not what we asked for.

I'm the mom who wanted a big family, at least five kids. But a miscarriage a year after my daughter was born messed up my insides and demolished any possibility of having another baby. To say I was crushed is an understatement.

My husband and I tried to adopt four times. And four times, it fell through for one reason or another. My hope of having a big family collapsed. But eventually, I realized that what I desperately wanted was not God's will for my life. Then I knew it was my choice. I could surrender my dream or stay miserable. It makes sense today because age gives perspective, but it made no sense then.

There is such a thing as wrong hope, as we put our hope in a future that can't be had, allowing ourselves to remain heart-broken because our dreams haven't come true. We can sometimes choose our paths, but sometimes our paths are chosen for us. We don't want to hope for something that isn't God's plan for our lives.

As God begins to reveal your personal act two, make an effort to surrender your vision for the future and lean on His. You can trust Him with all your hopes and dreams.

Journal Prompt:

Reflect on a moment when you had to surrender your dream to His wisdom.

Prayer Starter:

Lord, thank You for Your unfailing love and faithfulness. Help me to remember Your goodness and trust You with whatever is to come...

Day 31
Hope for the Future

Scripture Reflection:

For we are God's handiwork, created in Christ Jesus to do good works, which God prepared in advance for us to do. Ephesians 2:10

Encouraging Thought:

You are uniquely crafted by God *with* a purpose and *for* a purpose. Your empty nest is an opportunity to discover how He wants to use your gifts and experiences to make an impact.

The world will try to tell you that life is winding down, your job is done, and it's time to step back. But God's economy doesn't work like that. Every single season of our lives has substance, and each chapter is intentionally written.

Think about Sarah, Abraham's wife. She saw God's incredible faithfulness when He answered her prayer for a son at ninety years old. Or what about Naomi, Ruth's mother-in-law? She thought her story was over, but because of Naomi's faithfulness, Ruth became part of the lineage of Christ. Or Anna, the prophetess, who spent her life worshipping and fasting as she waited expectantly for the Messiah and, at eighty-four, held Him as a baby after decades of waiting. Your story is far from over–it's not a chapter closed, it's a book still being written.

Make the coming years your opportunity to dream again and embrace new callings as you confidently walk forward, knowing God has more. Remember, God isn't only a God of assignments but a God promising abundant life. As you pour out what's been poured into you, you will find a resolve you didn't know you had.

God is still writing your story, one day, one year, one word at a time. And the next chapter is going to be beautiful.

Goal for Today:

Realize you were created for such a time as this. Your future beckons!

Common Obstacle:

Identity Loss

Overcoming the Obstacle:

The deep, aching question may remain: *Who am I now?* For decades, motherhood shaped every part of your life, giving you purpose, structure, and a heart so full it often spilled over in exhaustion, joy, and relentless sacrifice for your children. But when the nest empties, when the noise fades to silence, it can feel like a piece of you has been packed up and carried away with your children's belongings.

Here's what the enemy doesn't want you to know: God is not finished with you yet.

Yes, the role of motherhood shifts, but your calling remains. Your identity was never solely in being a mother—it has always been in being His child. And if you're still here, it means there's still a purpose, a mission, and a kingdom assignment waiting for you, ripe for the picking.

The challenge is learning to embrace this season instead of grieving it, to stop looking back and start looking forward. The God who filled your heart and hands with children will now fill them with new assignments, new dreams, and a fresh outpouring of His Spirit.

Hope begins when you surrender this next chapter to Him, trusting that your future is as rich and meaningful as the years you spent raising your children. The best is not behind you—it lies just ahead. God calls you to step forward, pour out, and embrace a future brimming over with purpose.

You are not forgotten, and you are not finished. You are called, chosen, and walking in the divine purpose of a faithful God who *always* has more.

The boundary lines have fallen for me in pleasant places; surely, I have a delightful inheritance. Psalm 16:6

Journal Prompt:

Take a deep look and answer the question, who am I now? Thoroughly examine it and honestly write what you believe. Next, what does God believe about you?

Prayer Starter:

Lord, I know I'm on this planet for a reason. Help me see the opportunities You've placed before me and walk fearlessly forward in Your plans...

Conclusion
A Journey of Hope,
Courage, and Trust

As you close this book, let your heart rest in the truth that this journey is not the end but a beautiful beginning. Like a bird taking flight from its nest, this next season is filled with endless skies of opportunity and the gentle breeze of God's guidance. Though the nest may feel empty, it is not barren. It is a sacred space where new dreams can mature, and your spirit can soar on wings of faith.

It may not feel like it right now, but your after party is a time to celebrate. Jesus holds your future in the palm of His hand, and at the right moment, He will unveil it to you. All you need to do is set down your worries and cares and take what He is offering from His hand.

You have been created for such a time as this, and He has equipped you with the courage to face every challenge. Trust Him to walk with you into the unknown. Like the sturdy branches holding your nest, God's promises are firm and unwavering, providing the foundation to spread your wings and seize your future.

Lean into His faithfulness and hold onto the lessons you learn as you march forward. The God who has guided you this far will never leave your side. When doubts creep in or the road feels uncertain, remember the truths you've reflected on here: He is your strength, your peace, and your anchor. Just as the nest remains a symbol of home, love, and provision, so does God's presence remain with you—a place of constant refuge and renewal.

Take heart, dear Mama, and trust the One who makes all things new. You are thoroughly known, deeply loved, and held securely in His hands. The skies ahead are wide with possibilities, and the best is yet to come. Your *nest* is His *"next."*

With love and faith,

Kate

About the Author

Kate Battistelli is the author of the bestseller, *The God Dare: Will You Choose to Believe the Impossible* and *Growing Great Kids: Partner with God to Cultivate His Purpose in Your Child's Life.* She's a contributing writer to Jordan Rubin's *Maker's Diet Meals, The (In)courage Bible for Women* and *The Spirt-Led Woman's Bible.* Her writing has appeared in *Guideposts, The Joyful Life magazine, The Better Mom, Mici magazine,* and more. Kate is one-third of the popular *Mom to Mom Podcast* and is an inaugural honoree with *She Leads Tennessee.*

As a young actress in New York City, Kate had a life-changing experience, going from understudy to starring as Anna in the Broadway National Tour of *The King and I* opposite Yul Brynner for more than 1,000 performances. Kate and her husband laid down their careers in the Broadway theatre in answer to their first "God Dare", moving out of New York City and into a life of homeschooling and home business.

She's been married to her husband Mike for more than four decades and loves living in Franklin, Tennessee near her daughter Francesca, son-in-law and seven amazing grandchildren. Kate's heart is to serve women of all ages by mentoring and encouraging them to step out of their safe space and into His irresistible future.